W9-AQB-325

Date: 1/28/14

J 597.962 DUN
Dunn, Mary R.
Garter snakes /

PALM BEACH COUNTY
LIBRARY SYSTEM
3650 SUMMIT BLVD.
WEST PALM BEACH, FL 33406

Snakes

Garter Snakes

by Mary R. Dunn

Consultants:
Christopher E. Smith, M.Sc., A.W.B.
President, Minnesota Herpetological Society
Gail Saunders-Smith, PhD,
consulting editor

CAPSTONE PRESS
a capstone imprint

Pebble Plus is published by Capstone Press,
1710 Roe Crest Drive, North Mankato, Minnesota 56003.
www.capstonepub.com

Copyright © 2014 by Capstone Press, a Capstone imprint. All rights reserved. No part of this publication may be reproduced in whole or in part, or stored in a retrieval system, or transmitted in any form or by any means, electronic, mechanical, photocopying, recording, or otherwise, without written permission of the publisher.

Library of Congress Cataloging-in-Publication Data
Dunn, Mary R.
Garter snakes / by Mary R. Dunn.
p. cm.—(Pebble plus. Snakes)
Summary: "Simple text and full-color photographs describe garter snakes"—Provided by publisher.
Audience: 005-008.
Audience: K to grade 3.
Includes bibliographical references and index.
ISBN 978-1-4765-2072-8 (library binding)
ISBN 978-1-4765-3485-5 (eBook PDF)
1. Garter snakes—Juvenile literature. I. Title.
QL666.O636D86 2014
597.96'2—dc23 2013007429

Editorial Credits
Jeni Wittrock, editor; Kyle Grenz, designer; Eric Manske, production specialist

Photo Credits
Alamy: Chris Mattison, 11, John Cancalosi, 19; Corbis: Joe McDonald, 15; Dreamstime: Jason P Ross, 1; James P. Rowan, 7; Science Source: E. R. Degginger, 13, Francois Gohier, 17; Shutterstock: Jay Ondreicka, 21, Joe Farah, 5, cover, Matt Jeppson, 9, vlastas66, design element (throughout)

Note to Parents and Teachers

The Snakes set supports national science standards related to biology and life science. This book describes and illustrates garter snakes. The images support early readers in understanding the text. The repetition of words and phrases helps early readers learn new words. This book also introduces early readers to subject-specific vocabulary words, which are defined in the Glossary section. Early readers may need assistance to read some words and to use the Table of Contents, Glossary, Read More, Internet Sites, and Index sections of the book..

Printed in the United States of America in North Mankato, Minnesota.
032013 007223CGF13.

Table of Contents

Wigglers and Splashers

Garter snakes wiggle through
tall grass and puddles.
They nap on rocks in the sun.
You might even see one
in your backyard.

There are more than 15 species of garter snakes. They live in North America. Garter snakes live in dens under logs, rocks, or wood.

Stripes and Spots

Garter snakes come in many sizes and colors. The biggest garter snakes are more than 3 feet (0.9 meter) long.

Garter snakes have slim, scaly bodies. White, yellow, blue, or brown stripes mark their scales. Some have spots instead of stripes.

Finding Food

Garter snakes look and smell for prey. They eat anything they can catch. Garter snakes often eat toads, frogs, small fish, and worms.

Growing Up

In summer, females have
up to 100 babies at a time.
The babies are born live.
Newborn garter snakes
take care of themselves.

In fall, some garter snakes hibernate for winter. Many snakes curl together in a den to keep warm.

Keeping Safe

Garter snakes often slide into water to hide from land predators. Hawks, raccoons, bullfrogs, and turtles eat garter snakes.

On land, garter snakes
give off a strong smell
to keep predators away.
Garter snakes live about
2 years in the wild.

Glossary

den—a small, hidden place where a wild animal lives

hibernate—to spend winter in a deep sleep

predator—an animal that hunts other animals for food

prey—an animal that is hunted by another animal for food

scaly—covered in many small, hard pieces of skin called scales

species—a group of animals with similar features

Read More

Halfmann, Janet. *Garter Snake at Willow Creek Lane.* Smithsonian's Backyard. Norwalk, Conn.: Soundprints, 2011.

Raum, Elizabeth. *Garter Snakes.* Snakes. Mankato, Minn.: Amicus, 2014.

Wallach, Van. *Garter Snakes.* Snakes. Mankato, Minn.: Capstone Press, 2009.

Internet Sites

FactHound offers a safe, fun way to find Internet sites related to this book. All of the sites on FactHound have been researched by our staff.

Here's all you do:

Visit *www.facthound.com*

Type in this code: 9781476520728

Check out projects, games and lots more at
www.capstonekids.com

Index

Word Count: 193
Grade: 1
Early-Intervention Level: 17